THE BUSINESS SUCCESS GUIDE TO DEER FARMING

Comprehensive Insight To Profitable Herd Management, Breeding, And Sustainable Practices For High-Quality Venison Production

RICHMOND HAMILL

Disclaimer

The information presented in this book is based on the author's personal knowledge and understanding of livestock management. The author is not affiliated with any association, company, business, or individual in the livestock industry. All content is provided for informational purposes only and should not be considered as professional advice. Readers are encouraged to seek professional guidance and conduct their own research before making any decisions based on the information contained in this book. The author and publisher disclaim any liability for any adverse effects or consequences resulting from the use of the information contained herein.

Table of Contents

ABOUT THIS BOOK

This book "Deer Farming" is an invaluable resource for anyone interested in establishing or enhancing a deer farming operation. It provides a comprehensive exploration of the field, from foundational concepts to advanced practices, ensuring readers gain a thorough understanding of this dynamic and rewarding industry.

The importance of deer farming is underscored by its potential benefits, which include profitable revenue streams from venison, antlers, and velvet, as well as opportunities for environmental stewardship and biodiversity conservation. This book delves into these benefits, highlighting how deer farming can be a sustainable and lucrative venture when managed properly.

Understanding basic terminology and concepts is crucial for newcomers to the field, and this book offers clear explanations of key terms and principles. By laying out an overview of its structure, This book prepares readers for an organized and systematic approach to learning about deer farming.

Key challenges and considerations are addressed with practical advice and real-world examples, helping readers navigate common obstacles and make informed decisions. From selecting the right deer species and establishing infrastructure to understanding legal requirements, this book covers every aspect needed for a successful start in deer farming.

This book thoroughly explores the fundamentals of deer farming, including behavior, biology, feeding, health management, and breeding practices. It provides detailed guidance on managing deer from birth through adulthood, ensuring readers are equipped with the knowledge to maintain optimal health and productivity.

Farm infrastructure is another critical area covered, with insights into fencing types, shelter requirements, watering systems, and handling facilities. These elements are essential for creating a functional and efficient farm environment.

Feeding and nutrition are pivotal to deer health and growth, and this book addresses various feed types, dietary formulations, and seasonal considerations. By understanding how to optimize feeding strategies, farmers can enhance the well-being and performance of their herds.

Health management is thoroughly examined, offering strategies for disease prevention, vaccination, parasite control, and emergency care. Recognizing and addressing health issues promptly is crucial for maintaining a healthy and productive deer population.

Breeding and reproduction are essential components of a successful deer farming operation. This book covers breeding cycles, techniques such as artificial insemination, and care for pregnant does and fawns, ensuring that readers can manage reproductive processes effectively.

Handling and transportation are addressed with an emphasis on safe practices, stress reduction, and compliance with regulations. Proper techniques and considerations for animal welfare during transport are crucial for maintaining the health and safety of the deer.

Marketing and sales strategies are discussed to help farmers identify target markets, develop effective marketing plans, and navigate the complexities of selling live deer versus processed products. Building strong customer relationships and understanding market trends are key to successful sales.

Financial management is a cornerstone of a profitable deer farming business. This book guides cost analysis, budgeting, revenue streams, and financial planning, ensuring that farmers can manage their finances effectively and make informed investment decisions.

Finally, This book looks to the future with insights into emerging trends, technological advances, environmental practices, and evolving consumer demands. By staying informed about these trends, farmers can position themselves for growth and success in the ever-evolving field of deer farming.

INTRODUCTION

Welcome to the world of deer farming, where the beauty of nature meets the practicality of agriculture. In this section, we'll delve into the essentials of starting and maintaining a successful deer farm. From understanding the basics to overcoming challenges, this guide aims to equip you with the knowledge needed to thrive in this unique venture.

Importance Of Deer Farming

Deer farming holds significant importance both economically and environmentally. Economically, it presents opportunities for sustainable income through various channels such as venison production, velvet antler harvesting, and ecotourism. Environmentally, deer farms contribute to wildlife conservation efforts by providing a controlled environment for breeding and nurturing deer populations.

Basic Terminology And Concepts

Before diving into the intricacies of deer farming, it's crucial to grasp some fundamental terminology and concepts. Starting with understanding the different deer species commonly farmed, such as red deer, fallow deer, and white-tailed deer, each with its unique characteristics and requirements. Concepts like herd management, breeding cycles, and handling facilities are essential for effective farm operations.

Overview Of This Book Structure

This book is structured to guide you through every stage of deer farming, from initial setup to ongoing management. Each chapter focuses on a key aspect of deer farming, providing practical insights and actionable steps to ensure your success in this rewarding endeavor.

Benefits Of Deer Farming

The benefits of deer farming are multifaceted. Beyond financial rewards, which can be substantial through venison sales and by-products like antlers, deer farming offers a fulfilling lifestyle immersed in nature. It promotes sustainable land use practices and contributes to biodiversity conservation by preserving and responsibly managing deer populations.

Key Challenges And Considerations

While deer farming offers numerous benefits, it also comes with its share of challenges. Understanding these challenges upfront allows for proactive management.

Factors such as disease prevention, fencing requirements, and market fluctuations can impact farm profitability and sustainability. By addressing these challenges through informed decision-making and strategic planning, you can navigate them effectively to ensure the long-term success of your deer farming venture.

CHAPTER ONE

Getting Started

Choosing The Right Deer Species

When starting a deer farm, selecting the appropriate deer species is crucial to ensure the success of your venture. Different deer species have varying requirements in terms of habitat, diet, and climate. For beginners, it's advisable to start with species that are well-adapted to your local environment and have established farming practices.

White-tailed Deer: White-tailed deer are a popular choice due to their adaptability and relatively straightforward care requirements. They are native to North America, making them a good fit for many regions. They require moderate-sized enclosures and are known for their hardiness.

Red Deer: Red deer are another excellent choice for farming. They are larger than white-tailed deer and are known for their impressive antlers. They thrive in a range of climates but may require more robust fencing and larger grazing areas due to their size.

Elk: Elk, also known as wapiti, are larger than both white-tailed and red deer. They require significant space and sturdy fencing. Elk are often raised for their meat, antlers, and hides. Ensure that your farm has enough space and resources to cater to their needs.

Mule Deer: Mule deer are another option if you are located in western North America. They are hardy and can adapt to various habitats, but they may need specific types of fencing due to their jumping abilities. Consider their needs carefully before choosing this species.

Selecting A Suitable Location For Your Farm

The location of your deer farm plays a significant role in its success. A suitable site should offer a balance of factors including climate, terrain, and accessibility. Begin by assessing your land's suitability based on these critical elements:

Climate: Deer are sensitive to extreme temperatures, so choose a location with a climate that suits the deer species you plan to farm. For example, if you choose to farm red deer or elk, ensure that your area has a temperate climate with enough shelter options to protect them from harsh weather conditions.

Terrain: Deer requires varied terrain to thrive, including areas for grazing, browsing, and shelter. Opt for land with a mix of open fields and wooded areas. This variety helps mimic their natural habitat and promotes better health and well-being.

Accessibility: Ensure that your farm is accessible for transportation of supplies, equipment, and eventual harvesting. Proximity to major roads or highways can facilitate easier management and reduce logistical challenges.

Water Source: A reliable water source is essential. Deer needs ample fresh water for drinking and, in some cases, for wallowing. Ensure that your chosen location has access to a clean and sustainable water supply.

Understanding Legal And Regulatory Requirements

Before establishing a deer farm, it is crucial to understand and comply with legal and regulatory requirements specific to your region. These regulations can vary widely depending on location, so thorough research is necessary.

Permits and Licenses: Contact local agricultural or wildlife authorities to determine the permits and licenses required for deer farming. This may include animal husbandry licenses, zoning permits, and wildlife permits.

Animal Welfare Regulations: Familiarize yourself with animal welfare laws to ensure your farming practices meet legal standards. This includes proper housing, nutrition, and veterinary care for the deer.

Tax and Business Regulations: Understand the tax implications and business regulations related to farming. You may need to register your farm as a business entity and comply with agricultural tax laws.

Record-Keeping: Maintain accurate records of your deer inventory, breeding programs, and health treatments.

This not only helps with regulatory compliance but also aids in effective farm management.

Setting Up Basic Infrastructure

Setting up the basic infrastructure of your deer farm is a critical step to ensure a safe and efficient environment for your deer. This includes fencing, shelters, and feeding systems.

Fencing: High-quality, sturdy fencing is essential to keep deer contained and protect them from predators. Fencing should be at least 8 feet high to prevent deer from jumping over and must be built with strong materials. Consider using electric fencing or double fencing for added security.

Shelters: Deer need protection from extreme weather conditions. Construct shelters that provide adequate cover from rain, snow, and sun.

The shelters should be well-ventilated, dry, and insulated to ensure comfort for the deer.

Feeding Systems: Set up feeding systems that are easy to manage and clean. You can use troughs or automatic feeders depending on the size of your farm. Ensure that the feeding areas are easily accessible and allow for proper sanitation to prevent the spread of disease.

Water Supply: Install reliable water systems such as troughs or automatic waterers that can provide constant access to fresh water. Regularly check and clean the water sources to ensure they remain free of contaminants.

Acquiring Initial Deer Stock And Genetics

Once your farm infrastructure is in place, the next step is to acquire initial deer stock and ensure good genetics for your herd.

Choosing high-quality breeding stock is crucial for the long-term success of your farm.

Source of Stock: Purchase deer from reputable breeders or farms with a proven track record of healthy, well-bred animals. Ask for health records and verify that the deer have been properly vaccinated and tested for diseases.

Genetics: Focus on acquiring deer with desirable genetic traits, such as good antler growth, strong health, and desirable behavioral traits. This will help improve the quality of your herd over time and potentially increase profitability.

Quarantine: Upon arrival, place new deer in quarantine to monitor for any signs of illness before introducing them to the main herd. This helps prevent the spread of diseases and ensures the health of your existing animals.

Breeding Program: Develop a breeding program to enhance the genetic quality of your herd. Work with geneticists or experienced deer farmers to select breeding pairs that will improve traits such as antler size, disease resistance, and overall health.

CHAPTER TWO

Deer Farming Basics

Understanding Deer Behavior And Biology

Deer farming requires a solid understanding of deer behavior and biology to manage a successful operation. Deer are prey animals with a natural flight response, meaning they can be easily startled. They tend to be more active during dawn and dusk, which influences their feeding and movement patterns. Observing these patterns is crucial for effective management and ensuring the well-being of the herd. Deer are social animals and prefer to live in groups, so it's beneficial to keep them in herds to reduce stress and mimic their natural environment.

Their biology includes a complex digestive system designed to process a variety of vegetation.

Deer are ruminants, which means they have a multi-chambered stomach that ferments food before digestion. Understanding this allows farmers to tailor feeding practices to meet their nutritional needs. Additionally, deer have seasonal changes in behavior and physiology, such as antler growth in males and seasonal breeding cycles. Recognizing these patterns helps in planning breeding, feeding, and health management strategies effectively.

Deer also exhibit specific territorial behaviors and social hierarchies. In a farming setting, it's important to manage these behaviors by providing ample space and environmental enrichment. Overcrowding can lead to aggressive behavior and stress-related issues. Ensuring that deer have enough space to move freely and exhibit natural behaviors will help maintain a healthy and productive herd.

Feeding And Nutrition Requirements

Feeding and nutrition are fundamental aspects of deer farming that significantly impact herd health and productivity. Deer have specific dietary needs that vary depending on their age, sex, and the time of year. A balanced diet for deer includes a mix of forage, grains, and supplemental feeds. Quality forage, such as clover, alfalfa, and high-protein grasses, should form the bulk of their diet. These plants provide essential nutrients and help in maintaining optimal health and growth.

In addition to forage, deer benefit from supplemental feeds that provide additional vitamins and minerals. During the growing season, they require higher protein levels to support antler growth and overall development. Providing a mineral supplement that includes calcium, phosphorus, and salt helps in maintaining bone health and overall well-being. During winter months, when forage is less available, providing high-energy grains and concentrated feeds is essential to meet their nutritional needs and prevent deficiencies.

Monitoring the condition of the deer regularly is key to adjusting their diet as needed. Weighing the deer, checking body condition scores, and observing their overall health will guide adjustments in their feeding regimen. It's also important to provide clean, fresh water at all times to support digestion and overall health.

Health Management And Common Diseases

Effective health management is crucial for maintaining a productive deer farm. Regular veterinary care and monitoring are essential to prevent and manage common diseases.

Routine vaccinations are important for protecting deer from diseases such as bovine tuberculosis and chronic wasting disease. Ensuring that your herd is regularly checked and vaccinated will help in maintaining a healthy and disease-free population.

Common health issues in deer include parasitic infections, such as internal worms, and external parasites like ticks and lice. Implementing a parasite control program, including regular deworming and treatment for external parasites, will help in keeping these issues under control. Additionally, managing the environment to reduce parasite exposure, such as keeping feeding areas clean and providing adequate shelter, is important for preventing infestations.

Observing deer for signs of illness, such as changes in behavior, appetite, or appearance, is crucial. Early detection of symptoms and prompt veterinary intervention can prevent the spread of disease and minimize losses.

Keeping detailed health records for each deer helps in tracking treatments and identifying patterns that may indicate underlying health issues.

Breeding Practices And Reproductive Management

Breeding practices and reproductive management are essential for maintaining a successful deer farming operation. Understanding the reproductive cycle of deer, which includes the rut (breeding season), is vital for managing breeding programs. The rut typically occurs in the fall, and timing the introduction of males to females is key to successful mating.

Proper record-keeping is essential for managing reproduction. Tracking the breeding dates, gestation periods, and birthing dates helps in planning and managing the herd. Deer have a gestation period of about 200 days, so planning for the birth of fawns and their subsequent care is crucial. Providing a suitable environment for pregnant females, including adequate nutrition and a safe birthing area, supports successful reproduction.

Handling fawns immediately after birth is important for their health. Ensuring that they receive colostrum within the first few hours of life provides them with essential antibodies and boosts their immune system. Regular monitoring of fawn health and development, including vaccinations and nutritional support, is necessary to ensure their growth and integration into the herd.

Handling And Transportation Techniques

Handling and transportation are key aspects of deer farming that require careful attention to ensure the safety and well-being of the animals. Proper handling techniques minimize stress and prevent injury.

When handling deer, using low-stress techniques such as gentle restraint and minimizing noise and sudden movements helps in keeping the animals calm.

Training in handling techniques is important for both deer and farm staff. Employing handling facilities designed for deer, such as chutes and pens, helps in managing the animals safely. Providing adequate space and designing facilities that allow for easy movement and minimal stress during handling is crucial.

Transportation of deer requires specific considerations to ensure their safety. Vehicles used for transportation should be equipped with appropriate containment and ventilation to prevent overheating and stress. Ensuring that deer are transported in a way that minimizes movement and provides adequate space helps reduce stress and prevent injuries.

CHAPTER THREE

Farm Infrastructure

Types Of Fencing And Their Benefits

Fencing is a critical aspect of deer farming, ensuring the safety of your herd and protecting them from predators. The choice of fencing material and design depends on the specific needs of your farm and the type of deer you are raising.

High-Tensile Wire Fencing: This type of fencing is popular in deer farming due to its durability and effectiveness. High-tensile wire fencing typically consists of multiple strands of wire that are tensioned to create a strong barrier. This fencing is resistant to sagging and can withstand deer collisions.

To install, you'll need to set up sturdy posts, usually made of wood or metal, spaced evenly along the perimeter. Then, attach the wire strands, starting from the bottom and working your way up. Ensure that the wires are tightly secured and check for any gaps or weaknesses regularly.

Electric Fencing: Electric fencing is another effective option, especially for keeping deer within designated areas. This fencing works by delivering a mild electric shock when the deer come into contact with the wire, deterring them from attempting to breach the fence. To install electric fencing, set up insulated posts around the perimeter and run the electric wires through these posts. Connect the wires to an electric fence charger, which will supply the necessary voltage. Regularly inspect the system to ensure it's functioning correctly and that there are no breaks or shorts in the wire.

Mesh Fencing: Mesh fencing, often made of welded wire or chain-link material, is another option for deer farming. This type of fencing is typically used for smaller enclosures or for areas where visual barriers are important. Mesh fencing should be tall enough to prevent deer from jumping over and strong enough to resist tearing. Installation involves setting up the posts and attaching the mesh to these posts, ensuring the mesh is tightly secured and free from gaps.

Each type of fencing has its benefits and drawbacks. High-tensile wire is cost-effective and durable, electric fencing provides an additional deterrent, and mesh fencing offers high visibility and security. Assess your farm's specific needs and choose the fencing type that best fits your requirements.

Shelter Requirements For Different Seasons

Providing appropriate shelter for deer is essential to protect them from harsh weather conditions and to ensure their well-being throughout the year. The design and features of the shelter should be adapted to the changing seasons.

Winter Shelter: During winter, deer require shelter that offers protection from snow, wind, and freezing temperatures. A well-constructed shelter should have solid walls and a roof to keep the deer dry and warm. Insulation can be added to the walls and roof to enhance thermal efficiency. The shelter should be well-ventilated to prevent moisture buildup, which can lead to health issues. Ensure that the shelter is large enough to accommodate all the deer comfortably, with space for movement and rest.

Summer Shelter: In the summer, the primary concern is providing shade and ventilation to prevent overheating. Shelters should have open sides or windows that allow for airflow while still protecting from direct sunlight. Roofs should be designed to block out the sun and keep the interior cool. The use of reflective or light-colored materials can also help reduce heat absorption. Providing access to shaded areas and fresh water is crucial to keeping deer hydrated and comfortable during hot weather.

Transitional Seasons: During the spring and fall, the shelter should be adaptable to changing temperatures. This means having adjustable features like removable panels or ventilation systems that can be modified as needed. The shelter should protect from rain and wind while also allowing for adequate airflow to prevent damp conditions.

Regular maintenance of the shelter is important to ensure it remains functional and comfortable for the deer. Inspect the shelter frequently for any signs of wear or damage and make repairs as needed.

Watering Systems And Their Maintenance

Proper hydration is vital for the health and productivity of deer, making an effective watering system an essential component of your farm infrastructure.

Automatic Waterers: Automatic waterers are a convenient solution for providing a constant supply of fresh water to deer. These systems are designed to refill automatically as the water level drops. There are several types of automatic waterers, including those that use float valves or pressure-sensitive devices. To install, place the waterer in a location that is accessible to the deer and connect it to a water supply line. Regularly check the system for clogs or leaks and ensure that the waterer remains clean to prevent contamination.

Troughs and Buckets: For smaller operations or areas where automatic systems are not feasible, troughs and buckets can be used. These should be made from durable, non-corrosive materials and be large enough to provide adequate water for all the deer. Place the troughs or buckets in shaded areas to prevent water from heating up in the sun. Regularly clean and refill the containers to ensure the water remains fresh and free from debris.

Water Source Management: If your farm relies on a natural water source, such as a pond or stream, ensure that the water is clean and accessible. Consider installing a pump or filtration system to keep the water free from contaminants. Fencing around the water source may be necessary to prevent deer from entering and causing damage or contamination.

Regular maintenance of the watering system is essential to ensure its effectiveness. Clean and inspect the system regularly to prevent issues such as algae growth or blockages. Ensure that the water supply is consistent and that all components are functioning properly.

Feeding Stations And Storage Solutions

Efficient feeding practices are crucial for maintaining the health and productivity of your deer herd. Properly designed feeding stations and storage solutions help ensure that the deer receives the right nutrients and that feed is kept in good condition.

Feeding Stations: Feeding stations should be designed to minimize waste and encourage proper feeding behavior. Raised feeders are often used to keep feed off the ground and reduce contamination from soil and manure. The feeders should be large enough to accommodate the entire herd and should have dividers or separate compartments to prevent dominant deer from monopolizing the feed. Position the feeders in areas that are easily accessible to the deer but protected from the elements to keep the feed dry.

Feed Storage: Proper feed storage is essential to maintain the quality of the feed and prevent spoilage. Store feed in a dry, well-ventilated area to protect it from moisture and pests. Use airtight containers or bins to keep the feed fresh and prevent contamination. Regularly check the stored feed for signs of mold or insects and rotate stock to use older feed first.

Supplemental Feeding: Depending on the nutritional needs of your deer, supplemental feeding may be necessary. Provide mineral supplements and other nutrients as needed, following the recommendations of a veterinarian or animal nutritionist. Ensure that supplemental feed is stored separately from regular feed and is kept in a clean, dry environment.

By implementing these practices, you can effectively manage the feeding and storage needs of your deer herd, promoting their health and productivity.

Handling Facilities And Equipment Essentials

Handling facilities are essential for the safe and efficient management of your deer herd. Proper equipment and facilities help ensure that routine tasks, such as health checks and breeding, are carried out smoothly.

Handling Pens: Handling pens are designed to contain and manage deer during various procedures. These pens should be constructed with sturdy fencing and have ample space for the deer to move around. The design should include features such as chutes or alleys to guide the deer into specific areas for examination or treatment. Ensure that the pens are easy to clean and maintain to promote good hygiene and prevent the spread of disease.

Gates and Chutes: Gates and chutes are essential components of a handling facility. Gates should be secure and easy to operate, allowing for efficient movement of the deer in and out of different areas. Chutes are used to confine the deer for tasks such as weighing, tagging, or administering vaccinations. Chutes should be designed to minimize stress on the animals and allow for quick and safe handling.

Equipment: Essential equipment for handling deer includes scales for weighing, syringes and needles for vaccinations, and grooming tools. Invest in high-quality, durable equipment to ensure its longevity and effectiveness. Regularly inspect and maintain the equipment to ensure it remains in good working condition.

Safety Considerations: When designing and using handling facilities, prioritize the safety of both the deer and the handlers. Ensure that all facilities are designed to minimize stress and injury to the animals. Provide proper training for handlers to ensure they can safely and effectively manage the deer.

By establishing well-designed handling facilities and using the appropriate equipment, you can efficiently manage your deer herd and ensure their health and well-being.

CHAPTER FOUR

Feeding And Nutrition

Types Of Deer Feeds And Supplements

When it comes to deer farming, understanding the different types of feeds and supplements available is crucial for ensuring the health and productivity of your herd. The primary types of deer feeds include:

1.   **Forage Feeds:** Forage feeds are the natural diet for deer and include grasses, legumes, and browse. These can be grown in pastures or provided as hay during winter. Forage should be high in fiber and offer a balanced array of nutrients to support deer health.

2.   **Concentrates:** These are commercially prepared feeds with a higher density of energy,

protein, vitamins, and minerals. They are designed to supplement forage and are available in various forms, such as pellets, crumbles, and cubes. Concentrates are particularly useful for deer in the growing or breeding stages as they help meet increased nutritional demands.

3.   Mineral Supplements: Mineral supplements are essential for deer to prevent deficiencies and support overall health. These supplements often contain key minerals like calcium, phosphorus, salt, and trace elements. They can be provided in blocks, loose mineral mixes, or mineralized licks.

4.   Protein Supplements: During periods of high nutritional demand, such as fawning or antler growth, protein supplements like soybean meal, alfalfa, or special protein pellets can help meet the increased needs. High-quality protein is crucial for muscle development and overall growth.

Selecting the appropriate type of feed depends on your deer's age, sex, reproductive status, and the season. A mix of forage and supplementary feeds generally provides the best results, ensuring that all nutritional needs are met effectively.

Formulating Balanced Diets For Different Stages

Formulating a balanced diet for deer involves understanding their specific nutritional needs at various stages of growth and development. The dietary requirements of deer differ based on age, sex, and reproductive status:

1.   **Fawns:** Fawns require high levels of protein and energy for optimal growth. Their diet should include a combination of high-quality forage and concentrates that are rich in protein. Offering a high-protein starter feed helps support rapid growth and development during their early months.

2.   Growing Deer: As deer transition from fawns to juveniles, their protein needs remain high, but their energy requirements increase. A balanced diet for growing deer should include ample forage with added concentrates to ensure they receive the necessary nutrients for proper bone and antler development.

3.   Breeding Deer: Pregnant and lactating do need increased levels of protein, calcium, and energy to support their health and that of their offspring. A diet rich in high-quality forages, supplemented with specific mineral and protein mixes, helps meet these increased needs. Bucks in the breeding season also benefit from a diet high in energy and protein to support antler growth and overall vigor.

4.   Mature Deer: For mature deer not in the breeding season, maintaining a balanced diet with adequate forage and moderate supplementation is

sufficient. Ensure they receive a consistent supply of minerals to support ongoing health and productivity.

Formulating these diets involves calculating the nutrient content of available feeds and matching it with the deer's requirements. Nutritional analysis tools or consultations with a nutritionist can help ensure accuracy.

Seasonal Feeding Considerations

Seasonal changes impact the availability and nutritional quality of forage, necessitating adjustments in feeding strategies throughout the year:

1.   Spring and summer: During these seasons, deer have access to abundant green forage, which provides high levels of protein and energy. However, it is still beneficial to provide supplementary

concentrates to ensure that deer are receiving a balanced diet, especially if the forage quality varies.

2.	Autumn: As forage quality begins to decline, especially in areas with colder climates, it becomes essential to increase supplemental feeding. High-energy feeds and protein supplements can help deer prepare for the winter months and support antler growth in bucks.

3.	Winter: Winter conditions often limit the availability of high-quality forage, making supplemental feeding crucial. Providing hay, high-energy concentrates, and mineral supplements helps deer maintain their condition and prepare for the upcoming breeding season. Ensure that feed is accessible and protected from snow and moisture to prevent spoilage.

4.	Transition Periods: During periods of seasonal transition, such as the shift from winter to spring, gradually adjust the diet to match the changing availability of forage. This prevents sudden dietary changes that could stress the deer.

By adapting feeding strategies to seasonal changes, you can help ensure that your deer maintains optimal health and productivity throughout the year.

Feeding Strategies To Optimize Growth And Health

Effective feeding strategies are vital for optimizing deer growth and health. Here are some strategies to consider:

1.   Feed Quality and Consistency: Ensure that all feeds provided are of high quality and free from contaminants. Consistency in feed quality helps prevent digestive issues and ensures that nutritional needs are consistently met.

2.   Feeding Frequency and Distribution: Provide feed at regular intervals to maintain a steady supply of nutrients. Distribute feed in multiple locations to reduce competition and allow all deer access to food. Automated feeders can help manage feeding times and amounts efficiently.

3.   Monitoring Body Condition: Regularly monitor the body condition of your deer to assess whether they are receiving adequate nutrition. Body condition scoring can help identify if adjustments are needed in their diet.

4.   Adjusting Feed Rations: Based on the deer's health and performance, adjust feed rations as needed. If deer are not growing as expected or if there are signs of nutritional deficiencies, consult with a nutritionist to modify the diet.

5.   Hydration: Ensure that deer have access to clean, fresh water at all times. Proper hydration is essential for digestion and overall health.

Implementing these feeding strategies helps maximize the growth potential and overall health of your deer herd, leading to better productivity and reduced veterinary costs.

Monitoring Deer Nutrition And Adjustments

Monitoring and adjusting deer nutrition is an ongoing process that requires attention and flexibility:

1.   Regular Health Checks: Schedule regular health checks for your deer to monitor their overall condition and identify any signs of nutritional deficiencies or health issues. Blood tests and fecal

analysis can provide valuable insights into their nutritional status.

2.   **Performance Tracking:** Keep records of deer performance, including growth rates, reproductive success, and antler development. Comparing these records with your feeding practices can help determine if adjustments are needed.

3.   **Feedback from Observations:** Pay attention to how deer are responding to their diet. Changes in behavior, coat condition, and weight can indicate whether the diet is meeting their needs. Adjust feed formulations based on these observations.

4.   **Nutritional Consultation:** Periodically consult with a wildlife nutritionist or veterinarian to review your feeding program and make necessary adjustments. Professional advice can help optimize your feeding strategy and address any specific issues your herd may be facing.

5.   Seasonal Adjustments: Regularly review and adjust feeding practices according to seasonal changes and forage availability. This helps ensure that your deer continues to receive appropriate nutrition throughout the year.

By actively monitoring and adjusting deer nutrition, you can maintain a healthy and productive herd, ensuring long-term success in your deer farming operation.

CHAPTER FIVE

Health Management

Common Diseases In Deer And Prevention Strategies

Deer farming, like any other form of livestock management, requires vigilance against common diseases to ensure the health and productivity of the herd. One of the most common diseases affecting deer is Chronic Wasting Disease (CWD), a fatal neurodegenerative condition that affects the brain and spinal cord of deer. Prevention strategies include maintaining a closed herd to prevent the introduction of CWD and ensuring that feed and water sources are clean and free from contamination.

Another common ailment is Hemorrhagic Disease (HD), which is caused by two different viruses: Epizootic Hemorrhagic Disease (EHD) and

Bluetongue Virus (BTV). These diseases often cause sudden deaths in deer, accompanied by symptoms such as fever, swelling, and bleeding. To prevent HD, it's essential to manage the deer's environment by controlling insect populations, as these viruses are transmitted by biting midges. Regular monitoring and maintaining a sanitary environment can significantly reduce the risk of HD outbreaks.

Foot-and-mouth disease (FMD) is another concern, especially in regions where it is prevalent. FMD affects the mouth and feet of deer, causing lameness and ulceration. Prevention includes strict biosecurity measures such as controlling access to the farm and using disinfectants to clean equipment and facilities. Early detection and isolation of affected animals are crucial to prevent the spread of FMD within the herd.

Vaccination Schedules And Veterinary Care

Establishing a vaccination schedule is critical in maintaining the health of a deer herd. Vaccinations for common diseases like CWD, HD, and FMD should be administered as part of a comprehensive health management program. A typical vaccination schedule involves administering vaccines to fawns at weaning age, with booster shots provided annually or biannually as recommended by a veterinarian.

In addition to vaccinations, regular veterinary check-ups are vital for early detection and management of health issues. A veterinarian can conduct routine health assessments, including physical examinations, blood tests, and fecal analyses, to monitor the overall health of the herd. Regular deworming, as advised by the vet, helps in controlling internal parasites and ensuring the deer are free from common diseases.

It's essential to keep accurate records of all vaccinations and veterinary visits. This includes noting the type of vaccine administered, the date, and any observed reactions. These records will be useful for future reference and help in tracking the herd's health over time.

Parasite Control And Treatment Options

Parasites can significantly impact the health and productivity of deer. Internal parasites, such as worms and coccidia, can cause weight loss, anemia, and decreased productivity. External parasites, such as ticks and lice, can lead to skin irritations, infections, and overall discomfort.

To manage internal parasites, regular deworming is necessary. This can be done using broad-spectrum dewormers that target a variety of worms. It is essential to follow a deworming schedule based on fecal egg counts, which a veterinarian can perform. Overuse of dewormers can lead to resistance, so it is crucial to use them judiciously and according to veterinary recommendations.

External parasites can be controlled through the use of insecticides and tick treatments. Ensuring that deer have access to clean, dry bedding and maintaining good hygiene in their environment can also help minimize parasite infestations. Regularly inspecting deer for signs of external parasites and treating any affected animals promptly is essential for effective control.

Recognizing Signs Of Illness And Injury

Identifying signs of illness and injury in deer early can prevent more serious health issues and improve recovery rates. Common signs of illness include lethargy, loss of appetite, and unusual behavior.

Observing changes in a deer's coat, such as dullness or thinning, can also indicate health problems.

Injuries are often evident through lameness or visible wounds. Deer with injuries may display signs of discomfort, such as reluctance to move or favoring one limb. Prompt attention to any injuries, including cleaning and treating wounds, and seeking veterinary care if necessary, is crucial for preventing infections and promoting healing.

Regular observation and interaction with the herd can help farmers become familiar with normal behavior patterns and physical conditions, making it easier to detect deviations that may signal illness or injury.

Emergency Response And First Aid Practices

Being prepared for emergencies and knowing basic first aid practices can make a significant difference in the outcome of an illness or injury. An emergency kit for deer farming should include antiseptics, bandages, wound dressings, and basic first-aid tools. It's important to have a plan in place for dealing with emergencies, including contact information for a veterinarian and a protocol for handling injured or ill deer.

First aid for common injuries involves cleaning wounds with a mild antiseptic and applying appropriate dressing. For severe injuries, such as broken limbs, it is crucial to immobilize the affected area and seek veterinary assistance immediately.

In the case of emergencies like sudden illness or suspected poisoning, providing supportive care such as hydration and warmth while awaiting veterinary help can improve the chances of recovery. Regular training on first aid and emergency procedures for anyone involved in deer farming ensures a prompt and effective response when issues arise.

CHAPTER SIX

Breeding And Reproduction

Understanding Deer Breeding Cycles

Deer breeding cycles are critical to successfully managing a deer farm. Deer are seasonal breeders, with their reproductive cycles largely influenced by environmental conditions such as daylight hours and temperature. The primary breeding season for most deer breeds is the fall, which is triggered by decreasing daylight. This period is known as the rut. During the rut, males (bucks) exhibit increased aggression and vocalizations to attract females (does).

To effectively manage breeding cycles, it is essential to understand the estrous cycle of deer, which typically lasts about 21 days. Does generally comes into heat for a short period within this cycle, lasting 24 to 48 hours. To maximize the chances of successful mating, it is crucial to monitor does closely during this time. Keeping detailed records of estrous cycles can help in scheduling mating and ensuring that does are bred at the optimal time.

Monitoring reproductive behavior is another key aspect. Bucks will compete for does, and their behaviors can indicate when a doe is in estrus. Observing these interactions can help in timing the mating process accurately. Additionally, using technology such as estrous detection devices can aid in pinpointing the optimal breeding window.

Breeding Techniques

There are several breeding techniques used in deer farming, each with its advantages. Natural breeding is the most traditional method, where bucks and does are allowed to mate in a controlled environment. This method relies on the natural behaviors and instincts of the deer but requires careful management to ensure proper pairing and timing.

Artificial insemination (AI) is another technique used to control the genetics of the herd more precisely. AI involves collecting semen from selected bucks and then inseminating does at the optimal time. This technique requires careful handling and timing, but it allows farmers to introduce desirable genetic traits into the herd and improve overall herd quality.

Another method is controlled breeding, which involves the use of breeding pens where does and bucks are placed together in a controlled environment. This method helps to monitor and manage the breeding process more closely, ensuring that each doe is bred by a selected buck and that the timing of mating is precise.

Pregnancy Care And Monitoring

Proper pregnancy care is essential for the health of both the doe and her developing fawns. Once a doe is confirmed pregnant, she should be provided with a balanced diet rich in nutrients to support her and the growing fawns. A diet high in proteins, vitamins, and minerals is crucial during pregnancy.

Regular health checks are also important. Monitoring the doe's weight, body condition, and overall health can help detect any potential issues early. Routine veterinary care, including vaccinations and parasite control, should be maintained throughout pregnancy.

Setting up a suitable environment for the pregnant doe is also critical. Providing a clean, comfortable, and stress-free environment will help ensure the doe's health and the successful development of the fawns. Ensure that the doe has access to fresh water and is protected from extreme weather conditions.

Birth And Neonatal Care

The birth of fawns is a critical period that requires careful attention. Typically, does give birth in a secluded area to minimize stress and potential predators. It's essential to monitor the birthing process to ensure that everything goes smoothly and to assist if any complications arise.

Immediately after birth, the fawns need to be cleaned and dried. Ensuring that the fawns stand and nurse within the first few hours is crucial for their survival.

Colostrum, the first milk produced by the doe, provides essential antibodies that help protect the fawns from diseases.

It is also important to monitor the fawns' health closely in the days following birth. Regular checks for signs of illness, proper feeding, and weight gain are essential. Providing a safe, warm, and quiet environment will help the fawns adjust to their new surroundings and thrive.

Managing Young Deer (Fawns) For Optimal Growth

Proper management of young deer, or fawns, is vital for their development and overall health. Providing a high-quality diet that meets their nutritional needs is crucial. This diet should include adequate amounts of protein, calcium, and phosphorus to support their growth and development.

Regular health checks and vaccinations are important to prevent diseases and ensure that fawns grow into healthy adults. Monitoring their growth rates and body condition can help identify any nutritional deficiencies or health issues early.

Socialization and environmental enrichment also play a role in the development of young deer. Allowing fans to interact with other deer and providing a stimulating environment can help them develop social skills and reduce stress. Ensuring that they have access to clean water and shelter will contribute to their overall well-being and optimal growth.

CHAPTER SEVEN

Handling And Transportation

Safe Handling Practices For Deer

When handling deer, safety and animal welfare should be your top priorities. The initial step is to familiarize yourself with the deer's body language and behavior. Deer are naturally wary animals and sudden movements or loud noises can easily startle them. Always approach them slowly and calmly, using a soft voice to avoid causing stress.

For safe handling, use proper equipment such as deer gloves, which provide a firm grip while protecting your hands from antlers and hooves. Deer can be unpredictable, so it's essential to have at least one other person assist you to ensure safety.

Always ensure that the handling area is secure, with high fences or gates, to prevent any accidental escapes.

When catching a deer, use a catch pen or a corral designed specifically for deer. These structures should have solid sides to prevent the deer from seeing outside distractions. Use a calm and steady approach, guiding the deer into a smaller area where you can handle them more easily. Ensure that any handling equipment is in good condition and suitable for the size of the deer.

Techniques For Stress-Free Transportation

Transportation is a critical aspect of deer farming that requires careful planning to minimize stress for the animals. Begin by preparing the transport vehicle well in advance. The interior should be clean, well-ventilated, and have non-slip flooring.

Ensure that the vehicle is large enough to accommodate the deer comfortably without overcrowding.

Before loading the deer, provide them with a calm environment to reduce anxiety. Use a familiar handler or caretaker to comfort the deer during the loading process. Train your deer to enter and exit the vehicle calmly by using positive reinforcement techniques. Gradually introduce them to the transport vehicle to help them become accustomed to it.

During transportation, monitor the temperature and ventilation inside the vehicle. Ensure the deer are not exposed to extreme temperatures or drafts. Regularly check on the animals to assess their well-being and provide water if the journey is extended. Avoid abrupt stops or sharp turns that could startle the deer or cause injury.

Loading And Unloading Procedures

Loading and unloading deer require a structured approach to ensure both safety and efficiency. Begin by preparing the loading area with secure fencing and a ramp or chute that guides the deer into the transport vehicle. The ramp should be non-slip and gently sloped to make it easier for the deer to walk up and down.

When loading, use calm and slow movements to encourage the deer to enter the vehicle. Use a gentle push or guide them with a handler's presence to avoid startling them. Always have a second person assist in guiding the deer and ensuring they enter the vehicle smoothly.

For unloading, reverse the loading process. Open the vehicle doors slowly and allow the deer to exit at their own pace.

Avoid forcing them out of the vehicle, as this can cause stress and injury. Ensure the unloading area is secure and free from hazards that could cause the deer to panic or escape.

Regulations And Permits For Transportation

Deer transportation is subject to various regulations and permits, which vary depending on your location. Start by contacting your local wildlife or agricultural authority to understand the specific regulations applicable to your area. This may include obtaining a transportation permit or complying with animal welfare standards.

Ensure that your transport vehicle meets all regulatory requirements, including any necessary modifications for safety and animal welfare. Keep all relevant documentation, such as health certificates and transport permits, readily available during transportation. Failure to comply with regulations can result in fines or legal issues.

Regularly review and stay updated on any changes in transportation laws or guidelines. This will help you maintain compliance and ensure that your deer are transported in a manner that meets all legal and ethical standards.

Ensuring Animal Welfare During Handling And Transport

Maintaining animal welfare during handling and transport is crucial for the health and well-being of your deer. Start by providing a stress-free environment and handling the deer with care to avoid physical or psychological harm. Use humane and low-stress techniques during all interactions with the deer.

Regularly check the condition of the deer during transport, looking for signs of stress or discomfort. Provide adequate ventilation, hydration, and appropriate temperature control to ensure a comfortable journey. If any signs of distress or health issues are observed, take immediate action to address them, including seeking veterinary assistance if necessary.

After transportation, provide the deer with a quiet and comfortable area to recover from the journey. Monitor their behavior and health closely for any signs of illness or stress. Ensuring a smooth and stress-free handling and transport process will contribute significantly to the overall well-being and productivity of your deer.

CHAPTER EIGHT

Marketing And Identifying Target Markets For Deer Products

To effectively market deer products, identifying the right target markets is crucial. Start by analyzing the types of deer products you will offer—such as venison, antlers, or hides—and determine which markets are most likely to be interested in these products. For instance, venison is often sought by health-conscious consumers and gourmet chefs due to its lean, high-protein profile. Research local and regional food trends to find restaurants or food festivals that might be interested in offering venison as a unique option on their menu.

Next, consider the demand for antlers and hides, which are often used in crafts, jewelry, and home decor. Identify craft shops, online retailers, and artisans who might be potential buyers.

Building relationships with these buyers can be beneficial, so networking at trade shows and industry events can provide valuable contacts.

Lastly, evaluate the potential for selling directly to consumers through farmers' markets, local fairs, or online platforms. Setting up a booth at these venues allows you to connect with consumers interested in specialty meats and products. Ensure you understand the regulations and permits required for direct sales in your area to operate legally and efficiently.

Developing A Marketing Plan For Your Farm

Creating a comprehensive marketing plan involves several steps to ensure your farm reaches its target audience effectively. Start by defining your farm's unique selling points. What sets your deer farm apart from others? It could be organic practices, sustainable farming, or premium-quality products. Highlight these unique aspects in your marketing materials.

Develop a brand identity that reflects your farm's values and mission. This includes designing a memorable logo, choosing a color scheme, and crafting a compelling tagline. Consistency across all marketing channels—such as your website, social media, and packaging—helps build brand recognition and trust.

Next, outline your marketing strategies. Utilize a mix of online and offline channels to reach potential customers. This might include social media advertising, email marketing, and search engine optimization for your website, as well as traditional methods like flyers and local newspaper ads. Regularly assess the effectiveness of each strategy and adjust your plan based on the results and feedback from your target audience.

Selling Live Deer Vs. Processed Products

Deciding whether to sell live deer or processed products depends on your target market and resources. Selling live deer typically involves working with buyers who are interested in raising deer themselves or hunting enthusiasts looking for specific breeds. This approach requires knowledge of the regulations surrounding live animal sales, transportation logistics, and health inspections.

On the other hand, selling processed products involves a more complex setup but can offer higher margins. To process deer, you'll need to either set up a processing facility on your farm or partner with a licensed processor. This includes slaughtering, butchering, and packaging the meat according to health and safety regulations. Processed products can include various cuts of meat, sausages, and specialty items.

Consider the benefits and challenges of each option. Selling processed products provides more control over product quality and branding but requires additional infrastructure and adherence to stringent health regulations. Conversely, selling live deer may have lower overhead costs but demands effective marketing to attract buyers who prefer live animals.

Pricing Strategies And Market Trends

Pricing your deer products competitively involves understanding both production costs and market trends. Begin by calculating the cost of raising and processing deer, including feed, veterinary care, labor, and facility expenses. Ensure your pricing covers these costs while providing a reasonable profit margin.

Research current market trends to set competitive prices. This can be done by analyzing the prices of similar products from other deer farms or specialty meat providers. Pay attention to seasonal fluctuations and consumer demand. For instance, venison prices might rise during hunting season or around the holidays.

Additionally, consider offering different pricing tiers to appeal to a broader audience. For example, you might offer bulk purchase discounts, subscription models for regular deliveries, or premium pricing for specialty cuts. Regularly review and adjust your pricing strategy based on market changes and feedback from customers.

Building Customer Relationships And Brand Loyalty

Building strong customer relationships is key to ensuring repeat business and fostering brand loyalty. Start by providing exceptional customer service at every interaction, from initial inquiries to post-purchase follow-ups. Personalized communication and responsiveness can make a significant difference in customer satisfaction.

Encourage feedback and actively listen to your customer's needs and preferences. Implementing their suggestions and addressing any concerns can help improve your products and services. Consider creating a loyalty program or offering special promotions to reward repeat customers and incentivize referrals.

Engage with your customers through regular updates via newsletters, social media, or a blog. Share behind-the-scenes content about your farm, tips on using deer products, and information about upcoming events or promotions. This ongoing engagement helps keep your brand top-of-mind and strengthens the connection between your farm and its customers.

CHAPTER NINE

Financial Management

Cost Analysis And Budgeting For A Deer Farm

Effective cost analysis and budgeting are crucial for the successful operation of a deer farm. Start by listing all potential expenses, which include initial capital costs, operational costs, and maintenance costs. Initial capital costs encompass the purchase of deer, fencing, shelter, and other essential infrastructure. Operational costs include feed, veterinary care, labor, and utilities. Maintenance costs cover repairs and ongoing improvements to facilities.

Begin by estimating the cost of setting up your farm. This includes constructing deer enclosures, installing water systems, and setting up feed storage.

Allocate funds for the initial stock purchase and ensure you have enough reserves to cover the first few months of operational costs. Next, draft a monthly budget that accounts for recurring expenses such as feed, veterinary services, and labor. It's beneficial to use budgeting software or spreadsheets to keep track of these expenses accurately.

To refine your budget, regularly review actual expenses against your projections. This helps identify areas where costs may be exceeding expectations, allowing you to make necessary adjustments. Conducting a thorough cost analysis will help ensure that you have allocated your resources efficiently and are prepared for unexpected costs.

Revenue Streams (Meat, Antlers, Velvet, Breeding Stock)

Diversifying your revenue streams is essential for maximizing profitability on a deer farm. The primary revenue sources include meat, antlers, velvet, and breeding stock.

1.   Meat: Venison is a popular product that can provide a steady income. To maximize profitability, focus on breeding high-quality deer with desirable meat characteristics. Proper processing and marketing are key; ensure that you comply with local regulations and invest in quality processing equipment or services.

2.   Antlers: Antlers can be harvested and sold, especially if you have deer with impressive antler racks. They can be sold as trophies or used in various products such as décor or natural health supplements.

Keeping accurate records of antler growth and understanding market demand can help you optimize this revenue stream.

3.	Velvet: Deer velvet, the soft antler tissue, is sought after for its medicinal properties. Harvesting velvet requires specific techniques and timing. Invest in proper handling equipment and ensure you have a market for this product. Velvet is often harvested during the growth phase and requires careful processing to maintain quality.

4.	Breeding Stock: Selling breeding stock can be a significant source of revenue. Focus on developing a herd with desirable traits and maintain detailed records of lineage and performance. Market your breeding stock to other deer farmers or breeders, emphasizing the genetic advantages and health of your animals.

Financial Planning For Seasonal Variations

Seasonal variations can impact your deer farm's financial stability. Plan for these changes by analyzing historical data and forecasting future trends. For example, feed costs may fluctuate with seasonal availability, and certain times of the year may see higher veterinary expenses due to health issues or breeding cycles.

Create a financial buffer to cover periods of lower income or higher expenses. This can be achieved by setting aside a portion of your income during peak times. Consider implementing strategies to stabilize income, such as diversified revenue streams or value-added products. Regularly review and adjust your financial plans to account for any unexpected changes in the market or operational costs.

Investment Considerations (Equipment, Infrastructure)

Investing wisely in equipment and infrastructure is crucial for the long-term success of your deer farm. Start by evaluating your current needs and future growth plans. Key investments include fencing, feeding systems, water management, and shelter. Ensure that all equipment and infrastructure meet the standards for deer care and management.

When investing in equipment, prioritize durability and efficiency. For example, invest in high-quality fencing that will withstand the elements and minimize escape risks. Similarly, consider advanced feeding systems that reduce labor and waste. Infrastructure investments should focus on improving the overall health and productivity of your herd.

Evaluate the return on investment (ROI) for each major expenditure. This means considering how the investment will improve efficiency or increase revenue. Regular maintenance of equipment and infrastructure will also help extend their lifespan and reduce long-term costs.

Record-Keeping And Financial Reporting

Accurate record-keeping and financial reporting are vital for managing a successful deer farm. Start by establishing a system to track all financial transactions, including income, expenses, and investments. Use accounting software or spreadsheets to organize and analyze this data regularly.

Maintain detailed records of herd management, including breeding, health treatments, and growth metrics.

This information is crucial for evaluating the performance of your herd and making informed decisions. Regularly review your financial reports to monitor your farm's financial health, identify trends, and make necessary adjustments.

Consider working with a financial advisor or accountant who specializes in agricultural businesses. They can help you navigate complex financial issues, optimize tax strategies, and ensure compliance with regulations. Regularly updating and reviewing your financial records will help you maintain control over your farm's financial performance and support long-term success.

CHAPTER TEN

Future Trends In Deer Farming

Advances In Deer Farming Technology

Recent technological advancements have significantly transformed deer farming, making it more efficient and productive. One of the key innovations is the use of automated feeding systems. These systems ensure that deer receive a precise amount of feed at regular intervals, which optimizes their growth and reduces feed wastage. Automated feeders can be programmed to dispense different types of feed based on the nutritional needs of the deer at various stages of their growth. This not only improves the health and productivity of the herd but also simplifies the feeding process for farmers.

Another technological advancement is the implementation of electronic monitoring systems. These systems use GPS and RFID tags to track the movement and health of each deer. By collecting data on their location, behavior, and physical condition, farmers can quickly identify and address any health issues or changes in behavior. This real-time monitoring enables more proactive management, reducing the risk of disease outbreaks and improving overall herd management.

Additionally, advancements in genetics and breeding technology have led to the development of more efficient breeding programs. Genetic testing allows farmers to select deer with desirable traits, such as improved antler growth or disease resistance. By using this data to guide breeding decisions, farmers can enhance the quality of their herd over time, leading to better yields and higher profitability.

Environmental Sustainability Practices

Environmental sustainability is becoming increasingly important in deer farming. One key practice is the implementation of rotational grazing systems. This method involves dividing the pasture into smaller sections and rotating the deer between them. This approach prevents overgrazing, allows pasture plants to recover, and improves soil health. By maintaining healthy pastures, farmers can reduce erosion, increase biodiversity, and enhance the overall sustainability of their operations.

Another important practice is the use of waste management systems. Deer produces a significant amount of manure, which can be a valuable resource when managed properly. Composting manure and using it as a natural fertilizer reduces the need for chemical fertilizers and improves soil fertility.

Additionally, some farms are exploring biogas production from manure, which can provide a renewable source of energy for the farm.

Water management is also crucial for sustainability. Implementing rainwater harvesting systems and efficient irrigation practices can help conserve water resources. Providing clean, fresh water to the deer is essential for their health, and efficient water management ensures that this need is met without unnecessary waste. By adopting these sustainable practices, deer farmers can reduce their environmental footprint and contribute to a more sustainable agricultural system.

Consumer Trends And Market Demands

Consumer trends are shaping the deer farming industry in several ways. There is a growing demand for venison as a lean, high-protein alternative to traditional meats. This trend is driven by increased health consciousness among consumers, who are looking for healthier meat options with lower fat content. Deer farmers can capitalize on this demand by focusing on the quality and health benefits of their products, including emphasizing the natural and free-range aspects of their farming practices.

Another trend is the increasing interest in gourmet and specialty products. Consumers are willing to pay a premium for high-quality venison cuts, processed products, and unique offerings such as deer antler velvet or deer hide. By diversifying their product range and exploring value-added products, farmers can tap into niche markets and increase their profitability.

Sustainability is also a significant factor in consumer decision-making. Many consumers are looking for products that are produced in an environmentally friendly and ethical manner. Deer farmers who adopt sustainable practices and can demonstrate their commitment to environmental stewardship may find a competitive advantage in the market. Building a strong brand around sustainability and transparency can attract environmentally conscious consumers and enhance marketability.

Regulatory Changes And Their Impact

Regulatory changes can have a substantial impact on deer farming operations. Compliance with animal welfare regulations is essential, as these rules are designed to ensure the humane treatment of deer. Farmers must stay informed about changes in regulations related to housing, feed, and veterinary care to avoid potential legal issues and ensure the well-being of their herd.

Biosecurity measures are another area where regulations can affect deer farming. Strict biosecurity protocols are necessary to prevent the spread of diseases, especially those that can affect wildlife and livestock. Farmers need to be aware of regulations regarding disease reporting, movement restrictions, and vaccination requirements to protect their herd and comply with legal standards.

Additionally, regulations regarding land use and environmental impact can influence deer farming practices. Farmers may need to adhere to specific guidelines for waste management, water use, and land conservation. Staying updated on these regulations and implementing practices that meet or exceed requirements can help avoid penalties and support the long-term sustainability of the farm.

Opportunities For Diversification And Growth

Diversification is a key strategy for growth in deer farming. Farmers can explore various avenues, such as developing value-added products like venison jerky, sausages, or specialty cuts. By processing their meat, farmers can capture a larger share of the market and increase profitability. Additionally, offering products like deer antler velvet, which is used in supplements and traditional medicine, can open up new revenue streams.

Another opportunity for growth is agritourism. Farms can attract visitors by offering tours, educational workshops, or interactive experiences related to deer farming. This not only provides additional income but also raises awareness about the industry and creates a connection between consumers and the source of their food.

Collaborating with local businesses and restaurants can also lead to growth. By establishing partnerships and supplying venison to local markets, farmers can expand their customer base and increase demand for their products. Building strong relationships with local chefs and retailers can enhance market visibility and drive sales.

Exploring export opportunities is another avenue for growth. With increasing global interest in high-quality, specialty meats, farmers may find new markets for their products beyond their local region. Researching international markets and understanding export regulations can help farmers tap into global demand and expand their business.

By embracing these trends and opportunities, deer farmers can position themselves for long-term success and growth in an evolving industry.

Frequently Asked A Question And Their Answers

What is deer farming?

Deer farming involves raising deer for their meat, antlers, hides, and other products. It's similar to other types of livestock farming but specifically focuses on deer.

What are the main breeds of deer raised in farming?

The most common breeds include the Whitetail Deer, Red Deer, Sika Deer, and Elk (also known as wapiti).

What is the primary purpose of deer farming?

Deer farming can serve several purposes, including meat production (venison), antler production (for velvet or trophies), and hide production (for leather).

What kind of facilities are needed for deer farming?

Facilities typically include fenced enclosures to keep the deer secure, shelters to protect them from harsh weather, and facilities for feeding, watering, and medical care.

How much land is required for a deer farm?

The amount of land needed can vary depending on the number of deer and the farming practices. Generally, 5-10 acres per 10 deer is recommended, though this can vary.

What do deer eat?

Deer are herbivores and typically eat grasses, leaves, fruits, and vegetables. In farming, they might be fed a balanced diet of grains, hay, and supplements to ensure proper nutrition.

How do you manage deer health on a farm?

Regular health checks, vaccinations, and parasite control are essential. Providing clean water, proper nutrition, and maintaining a clean environment also help prevent diseases.

What are the common diseases in deer farming?

Common diseases include Chronic Wasting Disease (CWD), Epizootic Hemorrhagic Disease (EHD), and various parasitic infections.

How is breeding managed in deer farming?

Breeding is usually managed by selecting healthy, genetically diverse animals. Controlled mating and monitoring of pregnancy and birth are essential for successful breeding.

What is velvet antler, and why is it valuable?

The velvet antler is the soft, growing antler covered in velvet that male deer shed annually.

It's valuable in some cultures for its supposed medicinal properties and is often used in supplements.

How often do deer shed their antlers?

Deer shed their antlers annually, typically in late winter or early spring. New antlers begin to grow soon after the old ones are shed.

What are the legal requirements for deer farming?

Legal requirements vary by location but generally include permits for animal husbandry, adherence to zoning laws, and compliance with wildlife and agricultural regulations.

How do you prevent deer from escaping their enclosure?

Fencing is crucial for preventing escapes. Fences should be high enough (at least 8 feet) and made of sturdy material. Regular inspections and maintenance are also important.

What are the benefits of deer farming?

Benefits include a diverse income from meat, antlers, and hides, lower feed costs compared to some livestock, and the ability to manage a wildlife conservation area.

How is venison processed?

Venison is processed similarly to other meats, involving butchering, aging, and preparing for sale. It can be sold as steaks, ground meat, or processed into other products.

What are the challenges of deer farming?

Challenges include managing deer health, preventing escapes, dealing with predators, and complying with regulations. Additionally, deer can be more sensitive to changes in their environment.

How do you manage deer in different seasons?

In winter, provide shelter and extra feed. In summer, ensure access to shade and fresh water. Seasonal management also involves adjusting feeding practices and health checks.

Can deer farming be profitable?

Yes, it can be profitable, but success depends on factors like market demand, management practices, and initial investment costs. Proper planning and management are crucial.

How do you market deer products?

Deer products can be marketed through direct sales, farmers' markets, specialty meat processors, and online platforms. Building relationships with buyers and understanding market trends can help.

What are some good practices for deer farming?

Good practices include proper fencing, regular health monitoring, appropriate feeding, good record-keeping, and adherence to regulations. Additionally, continuing education on deer management can be beneficial.

CONCLUSION

Deer farming has emerged as a dynamic and multifaceted agricultural enterprise, demonstrating significant potential for profitability and sustainability. As the global demand for venison, antler products, and other deer-derived goods continues to rise, deer farming presents a viable alternative to traditional livestock farming. This industry, characterized by its versatility and adaptability, offers numerous advantages, from environmental benefits to economic opportunities.

One of the primary benefits of deer farming is its minimal environmental impact compared to conventional livestock farming. Deer are browsers rather than grazers, which means they consume a diverse range of plant materials and are less likely to overgraze pastures. This browsing behavior helps maintain soil health and promotes biodiversity, reducing the need for chemical fertilizers and pesticides. Additionally, deer farming can contribute to sustainable land use practices, as deer require less feed and water than traditional livestock, making them a more resource-efficient option.

Economically, deer farming can be highly lucrative. The market for venison, antler velvet, and other deer products is expanding, driven by increasing consumer interest in high-quality, lean meat and natural health supplements. Furthermore, the ability to diversify income streams by producing a variety of products—from meat and antlers to hides and ornamental antlers—can provide farmers with financial stability and reduce market risks. The initial investment in deer farming infrastructure and stock may be significant, but the long-term returns can be substantial, especially for well-managed operations.

The success of a deer farming venture hinges on several factors, including proper management practices, animal health, and market positioning. Effective management practices, such as rotational grazing, regular health monitoring, and appropriate breeding strategies, are essential for optimizing herd performance and ensuring animal welfare. Additionally, understanding market trends and consumer preferences can help farmers position their products effectively and capitalize on emerging opportunities.

In conclusion, deer farming represents a promising and sustainable agricultural practice with the potential for significant economic and environmental benefits. As the industry continues to evolve, ongoing research and innovation will play a crucial role in addressing challenges and enhancing productivity. By embracing best practices and staying attuned to market demands, deer farmers can contribute to a more sustainable and profitable agricultural sector, ultimately benefiting both producers and consumers. The future of deer farming is bright, offering a pathway to greater agricultural diversity and environmental stewardship.

THE END